Fas

FASTING SUCCESSFULLY

A PRACTICAL GUIDE TO SEEKING GOD

DEREK PRINCE

FASTING SUCCESSFULLY

This edition DPM-UK 2018

ISBN 978-1-78263-563-5
Kindle 978-1-78263-565-9
ePub 978-1-78263-564-2
PRODUCT CODE B28

Derek Prince Ministries · www.derekprince.com

Set in Arno by Michelle Kaplan, Renana Typesetting

Contents

Part 1

1

What is Fasting?

The theme of this study is "How to Fast Successfully." This subject does not readily lend itself to a sermon, but rather to some practical teaching on various aspects of fasting. Many people ask: "How do I fast? How long do I fast? How often should I fast? How should I break my fast?" The purpose of this study is to answer these questions and to clear up some misconceptions about fasting.

I think it is good to begin with a definition of fasting. The definition I have used several times is: fasting is abstaining from food for spiritual purposes. Normally fasting is not abstaining from fluids, but only from solid food. Although there were occasions in the Bible when people did fast without food or without water for as long as forty days, for this study we will consider fasting as abstaining from food for spiritual purposes.

Many of the people who have asked, "How do I fast?" have been Christians and members of churches for many years. Yet, apparently no one has ever taught them about fasting, even though the Bible has much to say about the subject. Since most of these people know something about prayer, it may be good to begin by pointing out a parallel between fasting and praying. In the Sermon on the Mount in Matthew 6, when Jesus speaks first about praying and then about fasting, He uses similar language in talking about both topics. The main difference is that when He talks about praying He includes a pattern prayer which we call the Lord's Prayer. But I think there is a basic parallel between fasting and praying, and I'll point out two aspects of it.

We all know we can pray as individuals, and most of us are also familiar with praying in groups. Group praying we usually refer to as a prayer meeting. Individual praying is what we do when we're by ourselves. I believe there is the same distinction in fasting: there is group fasting, where people fast together; and there is individual fasting, where a person fasts on his own.

We are also familiar with two kinds of prayer: (1) regular prayer at a set time each day, and (2) special times of prayer when the Holy Spirit leads us to take extra time beyond our usual pattern of prayer for a special need. The same, I believe, is true of fasting. I think fasting should be a regular practice in the life of every disciplined Christian. But beyond those regular times of fasting, there are times when the Holy Spirit leads us to give additional emphasis to fasting.

So we see that there is a parallel between praying and fasting. Just as there is individual prayer and collective prayer, so there is also individual fasting and collective fasting. Just as there are normal patterns of prayer and there are times of special prayer, so there should be normal patterns of fasting in the life of every Christian and there should be special times of fasting as the Holy Spirit leads.

2

Should All Christians Fast?

If we go to the Bible and to the history of Israel and the early church, we find that fasting was a regular part of the life of God's people. Under the Old Covenant, Israel was required by God to fast collectively at least once a year on the Day of Atonement and on other occasions. There are also records of individuals who fasted – Moses fasted, David fasted, Elijah fasted, and many of the kings of Israel led their people in fasting. In the book of Acts, we have records of the early Church fasting together in groups for special needs. Particularly when they were sending forth apostles, but also when they were appointing elders in local churches, the early Church would collectively fast and pray for God's guidance. Reliable Church tradition and recorded history also tell us that for several centuries the early Church practiced fasting regularly on Wednesday and Friday of each week. These were the two days normally recognized for fasting.

The early Methodists under John and Charles Wesley regularly practiced fasting. It was a normal part of their procedure, although I find that many Methodists have never heard of it. In fact, John Wesley would not ordain a man to the Methodist ministry unless he would commit himself to fast every Wednesday and Friday until 4:00 P.M. In other words, Wesley regarded it as an absolutely normal part of any Christian minister's life and discipline. Personally, I believe that the restoration of this practice would change the lives of many ministries and ministers.

3

How Should I Prepare for a Fast?

The first thing that I would like to say about preparation concerns the mental attitude with which we go into a fast. This has a great deal to do with whether the fast is successful or not. I believe we should approach fasting with an attitude of positive faith: it is God's will for me to fast, and God will bless me when I do fast in accordance with His will. I believe it is God's will because Scripture reveals that it is. We do not need some special feeling or revelation about the fact that fasting is the will of God, because the Bible clearly indicates that it is. We do not need some special revelation that it is God's will for us to pray because it is plainly taught in the Bible. People who wait for a special revelation for something that is definitely stated in the Bible seldom get that special revelation and therefore miss the purpose of God.

Furthermore, I believe that God will reward us in fasting if we seek Him with right motives and in a scriptural way. The Bible clearly promises this. Jesus said:

> *"But you, when you fast, anoint your head and wash your face, 18 so that you do not appear to men to be fasting, but to your Father who is in the secret place; and your Father who sees in secret will reward you openly."*
>
> (Matthew 6:17–18)

That is a very clear promise. if you fast in the right way with the right motives, God will reward you openly. So if you fail to fast, bear in mind that you are depriving yourself of the reward, because God cannot give you the reward if you don't meet His conditions. The writer of Hebrews lays a basic principle for approaching

God and seeking anything from Him. Hebrews 11:6 states, "But without faith it is impossible to please Him, for he who comes to God must believe that He is, and that He is a rewarder of those who diligently seek Him." When we approach God, the Bible says we must approach Him on the basis of faith. There is no other basis on which to approach Him. Further, if we come to God on that basis, we must believe two specific things: first of all, that He is (that He exists) and, secondly, that God is a rewarder of those who diligently seek Him. if you diligently seek God, He will reward you – that is guaranteed! He may not always reward you exactly the way you might have expected to be rewarded, but there will never fail to be given a reward to those who diligently seek God.

In Isaiah 58, we also have a series of promises to those who fast according to the will of God. I think it is worthwhile just looking at some of these statements. The Lord promises that all of these results will follow if fasting is done in a way pleasing to Him:

Then your light will break forth like the
dawn, and your healing will quickly
appear;
then your righteousness will go before you,
and the glory of the Lord will be your rear
guard.
Then you will call, and the Lord will answer;
you will cry for help, and he will say: Here
am I.
If you do away with the yoke of oppression,
with the pointing finger and malicious talk.
(Isaiah 58:8–9, 11–12 NIV)

I have made a list of ten specific promises for those who fast according to the will of God:

- Light
- Health
- Righteousness
- Glory
- Answered prayer
- Continual guidance
- Satisfaction
- Refreshing
- Work that endures
- Restoration

To me, any Christian who does not desire those benefits is very foolish. They are specifically promised to those who fast in accordance with the will of God. When we begin to fast with a positive attitude of faith that we are doing what the Scripture teaches, that we are obeying the revealed will of God, and that God Himself will reward us, then we can expect the specific rewards that are listed in Isaiah 58.

We also need to have the right attitude toward our own bodies. Many Christians have a wrong attitude towards the body. They have the impression that the body is a necessary evil they have to live with and that it will be a good thing when they're out of it. in the meanwhile, they don't want to give too much thought or attention to the body, because the erroneously believe they are being unspiritual if they do. I don't find that the Bible teaches that attitude towards the body. I'd like to read to you just two verses in 1 Corinthians:

> *Or do you not know that your body is the temple of the Holy Spirit who is in you, whom you have from God, and you are not your own? For*

you were bought at a price; therefore glorify God in your body and in your spirit, which are God's.

(1 Corinthians 6:19–20)

The Bible teaches that the physical body is the temple of the Holy Spirit and that when Jesus died on the cross and shed His blood, He redeemed not only our spirits and our souls, but our bodies. He bought the whole of us with the price of His shed blood. We belong to Him entirely – spirit, soul and body. God has a very real interest and a very specific purpose for our bodies. The body is to be the temple of the Holy Spirit. it is to be the place where the Holy Spirit dwells. The Bible tells us that God does not dwell in temples made by hands (see Acts 7:48). We can build Him any church, any synagogue, any tabernacle we like, but God will not dwell there. God has chosen to dwell in the physical bodies of those who believe in Him. Thus, the believer's body has a very important function as a residence of the Holy Spirit.

I believe that it is pleasing to God that I keep that residence of the Holy Spirit in the best possible condition. it should be healthy and strong and able to do the things God wants done.

Furthermore, Paul tells us about our physical members in Romans 6:13: "And do not present your members as instruments of unrighteousness to sin, but present yourselves to God as being alive from the dead, and your members as instruments of righteousness to God" So the various members of my physical body are intended to be instruments (or an alternative reading is "weapons") that God can use. They do not belong to me; they belong to God. I am to yield them to God. now I think it is logical and obvious that God wants His weapons in good condition. He doesn't want them feeble and broken down. He wants our bodies to be healthy. He wants our members to be strong, effective, and active because they are the members of Christ and they are the instruments God uses for His purposes in the earth. in a certain sense, Christ has no body in the earth except ours. Our bodies are the instruments that He uses for His will in the earth, and I have become convinced that God expects us to keep our bodies strong and as healthy as we can.

I am convinced that fasting is a very practical way to make and keep our bodies healthy. I believe that many physical as well as other problems would be solved if Christians would learn to fast in a practical and healthy way. Part of what I'm going to teach is intended to help you fast with the maximum benefits to your body.

When I look at the way Christians in America treat their bodies, especially the kinds of things they feed them, I ask myself, "What shape would their cars be in if they treated them with as little understanding and as little respect as they treat their bodies?" I've come to the conclusion that most people's cars would not be running!

Our bodies are much more forgiving and long- suffering than our cars. Personally, I think it is simply common sense to treat your body with at least as much concern and intelligent care as you would treat your car. in fact, it should be more because $20,000 will buy a new car, but $20,000 will not begin to buy a new body. it can't even buy one eye. There is no monetary price to be set on a healthy body. One basic problem with Christians is that they simply don't appreciate the importance of a healthy body.

In regard to physical aspects of fasting, some people should exercise caution. If you have certain types of physical problems such as diabetes or tuberculosis, or if you are on some kind of regular medication, you should consult your physician for advice about whether you should fast. There are some people who cannot practice fasting. For example, those who are diabetics have to maintain their blood chemistry at certain levels. in such cases, I believe that it is the responsibility of other Christians to fast for those who cannot.

4

What Is the Purpose of Fasting?

Let's talk about choosing objectives in fasting. Somebody said once, "if you aim at nothing, you can be pretty sure you'll hit it." We need to have an aim or an objective when we go into something like fasting.

We can find many good, scriptural reasons for fasting. I'll give you some, relating them to myself. First, one biblical purpose for fasting is to humble myself. David said, "I humbled my soul with fasting" (Psalm 35:13 NAS). We need to bear in mind that humility is not an emotion; not something vague; but rather it is specific. God will not humble us because He has told us to humble ourselves. I have proved by experience that if I fast with the right motives and in faith, I can humble myself.

When I humble myself, God exalts me. That principle runs throughout the Bible. "And whoever exalts himself will be humbled, and he who humbles himself will be exalted." (Matthew 23:12). We have to make the choice. Do I want to be abased? Then I can exalt myself. Do I want to be exalted? Then I need to humble myself. I believe that the basic way for a believer to humble himself is by fasting.

Another motive for fasting is to come closer to God. The Scripture says that if you "draw near to God… He will draw near to you" (James 4:8 NAS).

A third reason for fasting is to understand God's Word more clearly. I have learned by experience over the years that when I'm seeking God in times of fasting, He gives me further, deeper understanding of His Word. Another very important reason for fasting is to find God's will and to receive direction in your life. Ezra said, "Then I proclaimed a fast there at the river of Ahava, that we might humble ourselves before our God, to seek from Him the right way for us and our little ones and all our possessions." (Ezra 8:21). Again, it has been my experience and my testimony that when I humble myself in fasting and seek Him for direction and guidance, He does lead me in the right way. I've proved this in many situations where we have had to move from country to country and when we have had to make decisions between going to one field or another to work, to one type of ministry or another. I've found that if we take time to fast and pray, in humility, seeking God's direction, we receive what we pray for.

Another very common reason for fasting is to seek healing. Isaiah 58:8 says, "Then your light shall break forth like the morning," This also applies to deliverance from evil spirits. Jesus said in one place about a certain type of evil spirit, "However, this kind does not go out except by prayer and fasting" (Matthew 17:21). Before Jesus Himself entered into His ministry of healing and deliverance, He spent forty days fasting.

We also can fast when we need God's intervention in some particular crisis, or when some tremendous problem has arisen which we can't handle by ordinary means. There are many examples of this in the Bible. In 2 chronicles 20, Jehoshaphat and the people of Judah found that they were facing an invading army which they could not meet with normal military methods. They humbled themselves before God, gathered together, fasted, and prayed. God dealt with the invading army. They didn't have to use a single weapon. God totally defeated their enemies for them and I don't believe God has any favorites. I believe He's just as willing to intervene on our behalf when we seek Him in the same way.

A final reason for fasting is to intercede and pray on behalf of others. Many, many people come to me about their unsaved relatives and they ask, "What can I do to get my relatives saved?" I often ask them, "Have you ever fasted and prayed for your unsaved husband or for your unsaved son or daughter? Are you willing to make a personal sacrifice – do something that will cost you – on behalf of your loved one?" There are many testimonies from believers of how God has answered the prayer that is accompanied by fasting on behalf of unsaved relatives.

If you're going to have a special period of fasting – more than a day or so – or you have some special purpose for fasting, sometimes it is good to make a written list of what you are fasting about and date it. I'm glad that many years ago in the early 1950s I did that on several occasions. I still have the lists. in looking back over them, I see with amazement how many of the things that I fasted for God answered – and some of them were great things. To give you one example, I fasted and prayed for the salvation of my mother, and though it took many years, God saved her very definitely and very dramatically almost at the last moment. At about the last time I could be reassured she really understood the Gospel, she had a tremendous experience of salvation, so it pays to pray and to fast. When I look back on those lists now, I praise God for the marvelous answers to prayer. A prayer list might be a good idea in your ordinary prayer life. That's not to say that everybody needs to do it, but if you do, one day you'll praise God for the way He's answered your prayers.

5

How Long Should I Fast?

Now we come to the question of choosing a length of time to fast. My advice is: don't begin with a very long fast. Don't begin with a week, two weeks, or forty days. Some people do, and they achieve it, but I find it's better to start climbing the ladder from the bottom, rung by rung. The problem is, if you start with too long a period and you don't achieve it, then you feel defeated. You may give up and never try again. I would suggest that normally it is better to begin at the bottom of the ladder and climb toward the top.

If you are not familiar with fasting, and you don't really feel equal to a big test, begin by omitting the last meal of the day. If you normally would eat your last meal about 6:00 or 6:30 P.M. and don't have any snacks afterwards until breakfast the next morning, you've actually fasted from lunch time to breakfast time, which is about 18 hours. That's quite a substantial period to be without food by only missing one meal. That way you achieve a real fast without too drastic a change in your life pattern or too great an objective. If you succeed in that, the next time you may want to skip the last two meals – the noon meal and the evening meal. If you don't eat until breakfast then you have actually been 24 hours without food. Then when you begin to feel like a real soldier, you can omit all three meals one day and you will have fasted from supper the previous night until breakfast the next day – about 36 hours.

Once you have achieved that and know you can do it, then I think it's time to seek the Lord as to whether He wants you to go on a longer fast. Again I would advise you not to take too big a step the first time. Take two or three days, or a week. If you spend a week fasting, that will probably have a substantial effect on the course of your life.

Looking back on my own career of ministry, I believe that if I had not practiced fasting many years ago, I would not be where I am today. I believe that fasting in many ways settled the course my life was to take. Again I come back to the Scripture that I quoted once already, "[God] is a rewarder of them that diligently seek him" (Hebrews 11:6). I say that not only on the basis of Scripture, but on the basis of personal experience! Now, it's perfectly possible to fast two or three weeks. In the Bible quite a number of people fasted for forty days, and I know a good many people who are alive who have fasted for as long as forty days. But I do not believe that it is wise to make the length of time your main objective. It isn't really as important how long you fast as that you fast in the will of God, that your motives are right, and that you get the benefits which should be yours from fasting.

To sum up, I suggest that you begin on a small scale and gradually increase the length of your fasts.

6

What Happens During a Fast?

I have already spoken about your mental attitude, which is probably the most important thing in fasting. now let's talk about what happens during a fast. This is an important section of our study, and there are a number of things I would like to suggest.

On a practical level, one important thing to do is to guard against constipation. if you know you are going to fast, make your last meal or two something which will prevent you from becoming constipated. everyone has his own particular way of arranging for that, but some obvious things you can do are to eat more than the usual amount of fruit, salad, fruit juice, or maybe a type of bran cereal. That's something you can settle for yourself, but it is a detail that you ought to take into consideration.

During a fast, I very strongly recommend that you take extra time for Bible reading and for prayer. I put Bible reading first because, in my opinion, it is wise to make it a practice not to pray without first reading your Bible. When you read your Bible, it anoints your spirit, and it gets your mind in line with God's thoughts.

Your prayer will normally be much more effective and focused after Bible reading.

If you are just fasting a couple of meals, you may feel that you do not have much time, but after all, you have the time you would normally have spent preparing and consuming two meals. Offer that time to the Lord. At least spend that time specifically in Bible reading and prayer.

Secondly, guard against spiritual attack. The real sacrifice in fasting is not going without food. Rather, it is the fact that when you really begin to seek God, pray, and fast for things that matter, Satan is going to turn extra spiritual forces loose against you. You may find that strange oppressions begin to come over you – doubt, fear, or loneliness. You may somehow feel yourself in a dark place – or you may lose some of the usual feelings of joy, peace, and happiness that you normally have as a Christian. Don't get worried if that happens. in fact, it's a kind of back-handed compliment from the devil. it means that you are worrying him, and he's out to prevent you from achieving your objectives. Don't yield to these emotions. Don't let feelings dictate to you. Bear in mind the great basic truths of the Word of God: God is on your side; God loves you and is a rewarder of those who diligently seek Him. This is true whether you feel it or not. Don't let feelings turn you away.

Another caution I would give is to avoid religious ostentation. I think we should look at Matthew 6:16. *"Moreover, when you fast, do not be like the hypocrites, with a sad countenance. For they disfigure their faces that they may appear to men to be fasting. Assuredly, I say to you, they have their reward."* Don't put on a religious act. Don't let everybody know that you are fasting. Some people will have to know, but don't make a show of it. Don't make a display of it. Do it as quietly and as unostentatiously as possible.

Generally speaking, you will be able to carry on your normal daily duties and activities. My wife once went on a prolonged fast – over four weeks – when we lived in London, and during all that time she prepared all the meals for the family and always sat with us at the table, although she did not eat. neither did she give up any of her other normal domestic activities. About the same time, I fasted for more than three weeks and still carried on my normal activities during that period. We used to hold five indoor meetings and three open-air meetings in our church every week at that time. I conducted and preached in every one of them. normally speaking, with a few exceptions, fasting does not prevent you from doing the things you would ordinarily be doing. in fact, after a while you may be able to do them much better when you're fasting than when you're eating.

I would caution you not to make a show of your fasting. Just carry on your normal activities as much as possible.

7

What About Unpleasant Physical Reactions?

Now we come to the question which always occupies people's minds – unpleasant physical reactions from fasting. Because of current life styles, most people will experience some type of physical reaction in the early stages of a fast.

Some common ones are headaches – and they can be very severe – dizziness, and nausea. I'm no medical expert, but people who study reactions from a medical point of view say that, in most cases, what is happening is that the blood in your body which is normally taken up in the process of digestion is now liberated from that and begins to work in other areas to clear them up. For instance, if you are a heavy coffee drinker, you will normally get quite a severe headache when you fast. That is the coffee drinker's penalty for all the coffee he drinks.

What most of us don't realize is that the process of digestion is very hard work. if you eat a heavy meal, much of your physical energy for the next hour or two is mainly taken up dealing with that meal. consequently, the blood that is there cannot be used in other areas of your body. For instance, I think it is a matter of experience that if you go swimming too soon after a heavy meal, you may get cramps in your arms or legs. Why? Because all the blood is in the stomach being used for the digestive process. But by the time your food is digested you can go swimming and you won't get cramps. in other words, the blood is liberated for other activities. if you're fasting for a day, you are liberating your blood to do a lot of cleanup jobs which badly need to be done, but which never are done when your blood has to spend its time digesting food.

In actual fact, to overeat is to reduce our physical energy. When you go beyond what you need in food, you are simply making your body do extra, unnecessary work digesting unneeded food. Then it isn't able to do the other things that need to be done. Personally, I have discovered by experience that I cannot preach my best after a heavy meal. I have to have at least an hour or two between a heavy meal and preaching because the blood isn't in my brain, it's in my stomach. My brain is fuzzy: it isn't equal to the job.

We said there may be various physical reactions from fasting in most people, especially in our modern way of life. If you can find the faith to do it, praise God for them. "Thank you, God, for my headache. I realize my blood is there doing something that needed to be done a long while ago!" Don't stop your fast. if you do, you have let the devil defeat you.

Daniel said, "I set my face unto the Lord God to seek by prayer and supplications, with fasting" (Daniel 9:3). When you fast, you need to set your face. You must make up your mind that you are going to do it. Don't leave open the possibility that you might have that meal after all because then the devil will be at you all the time to eat. if you have made your mind up not to eat again today and dismiss that possibility from your mind, it's much easier.

At mealtime you may feel real hunger pains. Actually, you really don't need food, but your stomach operates by habit. In about an hour, you will find the hunger pains will subside without your having eaten. it was just a habit. Your stomach was set like a clock to react that way at that time. if you want to fool your stomach take a couple glasses of water. When you fill your stomach up with water, it gets fooled. it thinks it has some food and stops protesting.

If these physical reactions become severe, you may have to give up everything else and lie down and rest. That is good for you, too. if you are in a position of employment where you can't do that, then you will have to choose another way or another day. if your reactions become so severe that you cannot endure them, then I would advise you to break the fast, take a little while to recover, and then try again. You may be quite surprised the next time. You'll hardly have any reaction.

Fasting uncovers both our spiritual and physical problems. When the problem is exposed, don't blame the problem on the fasting. instead, thank God that the fasting has revealed the problem which was already there. if your problems are severe – whether emotional, spiritual or physical – as a result of fasting, then I think you need to consult somebody with experience, either a pastor or physician.

8

How Can I Fast with Maximum Physical Benefits?

If you want the maximum physical benefits from your fast, there are certain things that will help you. I will give you some very practical suggestions to help you benefit the most from your fast.

(1) Get plenty of rest. In fact, take extra time to rest. You can pray just as well lying in your bed as you can on your knees.

(2) Take some exercise and try to get some fresh air. I find it very easy to pray when I'm walking;

and when I'm walking I'm getting fresh air and exercise – all three at once! It greatly increases both the spiritual and physical benefits of the fast.

Usually in most people's experience of fasting, the unpleasant reactions come to a climax in the second, third or fourth day. if you get beyond that, then you come into a period where fasting really becomes exciting, exhilarating, and enjoyable. You may even find that your physical strength increases remarkably. My experience, not so much in the physical, but with mental activity, is that when I get to that stage in a fast, I can do in one hour work that would normally take me two or three hours. My mind is much clearer, although my body may still be protesting a little with the sense of weakness.

(3) While you are fasting, it is normally wise to consume plenty of fluids, because that has the effect of flushing out your kidneys and generally cleaning out your body. What kind of fluids? Well, I've come to believe that the best thing is pure water – and I don't mean the water that comes out of the tap, but the purified water that

you can buy in the supermarket or from a firm that handles this product.

When you fast, you will invariably notice that your taste becomes much keener, and you will perceive all sorts of horrid tastes in the drinking water which you hardly noticed when you were eating – particularly the taste of chlorine.

Although I strongly feel that it is wise to take just pure water, at the beginning of your fast you may want to put some honey in the water. Take the water hot with a little lemon. Honey and lemon together are kind of purifying. if you don't feel that you want to stick to just water, there are various other fluids available such as broth, bouillon or fruit juice.

Personally again, I would advise people during fasting to avoid drinking tea or coffee since they both are very strong stimulants. You get more physical benefits from your fast if you do not consume these during your fast.

9

What Are the Different Types of Fasts?

There are times when God does lead us to abstain from fluids, but this can be a dangerous area physically. The only examples I can find in the Bible of people fasting extensively without food or water are Moses and Elijah, who each fasted forty days. However, they were on a supernatural plane – in the immediate presence of God or under some supernatural power. I don't believe that is a normal pattern for us.

I believe the pattern for the length of time without fluids is found in Esther 4:16. Esther said to her uncle Mordecai, "Go, gather all the Jews who are present in Shushan, and fast for me; neither eat nor drink for three days, night or day."

Three days, night and day is 72 hours, and personally I would not advise anybody to go beyond 72 hours without fluids. If you try 72 hours without eating or drinking, I think you will find that you'll be on your knees at the end – if not spiritually, at least physically. However, I must say that I have twice been 72 hours without food or drink, and God blessed me in it. I would not recommend anybody to go beyond this length of time. To do so, I believe, is very dangerous physically. I think any doctor would confirm that.

I just need to mention another practical physical detail at this point. While you are fasting, your bowels may not move, but if you have avoided constipation to begin with, you don't need to worry about that. When you resume eating, your bowels will start functioning again. if you start eating in the right way, you will find that you have probably cleansed your bowels considerably and that they are in better condition than when you started fasting. if your bowels don't move during your fast, don't worry. Sometimes they will; sometimes they won't. Obviously, if you are fasting for a considerable period of time and they have already moved, there would be no further need for them to move, since no food has been digested.

There is a biblical precedent for what I would call a partial fast. in other words, you eat something, but you don't eat much.

> *In those days I, Daniel, was mourning three full weeks* [that's 21 days], *I ate no pleasant food, no meat or wine came into my mouth, nor did I anoint myself at all, till three whole weeks were fulfilled* (Daniel 10:2–3)

That was not a complete fast, but it was what is called a partial fast. He didn't eat meat, and he didn't eat dessert – he just ate simple, basic food.

Daniel's fast was a kind of mourning. Fasting and mourning are very closely related in the Bible. There is a spiritual mourning which God has promised to bless

> *"Blessed are those who mourn, for they shall be comforted"* (Matthew 5:4 NAS).

There may be a time when you are led to a kind of partial fast, like Daniel.

A short time ago, I met a catholic priest, a missionary in Japan, who had just come from a place here in the U.S. where a group of priests were praying and fasting for forty days on behalf of all the priests. This really was exciting to me. Some of the priests had been there the whole forty days, but others, like the missionary from Japan, had just been there a week. They took time off from everything else and were praying and seeking God, asking Him to bless all the priests in the roman catholic church. He informed me that they were experiencing a tremendous blessing in this gathering. Let's bear in mind that none of this is out of date; it's all taking place today; and if the Protestants aren't doing it, then the Catholics are!

The incident just related brings up another point about fasting: if a group agrees to fast together, I think that if possible they should also meet together at least part of the time to pray and seek God as a group. There are things accomplished by praying together that often will not happen just by our praying on our own.

10

How Are the Sabbath and Fasting Related?

An important related facet of this message, which is slightly beyond fasting, is the matter of taking time for God. in the 58th chapter of Isaiah, we have already looked at the blessings that are promised to those who fast in accordance with the will of God. The first twelve verses of Isaiah 58 deal with fasting; the last two verses deal with keeping God's Sabbath, and I believe they are related. The following are the last two verses of Isaiah 58:

> *"If you keep your feet from breaking the Sabbath and from doing as you please on my holy day, if*

> *you call the Sabbath a delight and the Lord's holy day honorable, and if you honor it by not going your own way and not doing as you please or speaking idle words, then you will find your joy in the LORD, and I will cause you to ride on the heights of the land and to feast on the inheritance of your father Jacob." The mouth of the LORD has spoken."* (Isaiah 58:13–14 NIV)

I believe it is no accident that those two verses come immediately after the twelve verses on fasting. Let me say that I do not believe that Christians are required to observe the Jewish Sabbath, nor do I believe that Sunday is the Sabbath. I believe that Saturday is the Sabbath and that Jews are required to observe it; but Christians, not under the Law, are not required to observe that Sabbath. That is my personal conviction. in the epistle to the Hebrews, it says, "There remains therefore a Sabbath rest for the people of God" (Hebrews 4:9 NAS). The root idea of the Sabbath is resting and ceasing from our own activities. I believe that it is very profitable to unite together fasting with resting from our own works. The average American is either working, at home busy with his family, has a spare job, or is busy with some kind of recreation.

Actually, there is a tremendous spiritual blessing from just relaxing and waiting upon God and not being busy with anything. I find that this is a principle of the Bible. When God brought Israel into the Promised Land, He said, "every seventh year your land is to have a Sabbath. For one year out of seven don't sow it: don't do any work on the land; let it lie fallow" (see Leviticus 25:2–6). All the time Israel was in the land, they failed to observe that. So God warned them, "if you don't do it when you are in the land, I will turn you out of the land and the land will have its Sabbath while you are out of it." I want you to read that warning of judgment:

> *I will scatter you among the nations, and will draw out my sword and pursue you. Your land will be laid waste, and your cities will lie in ruins.*
>
> *Than the land will enjoy its Sabbath years all the time that it lies desolate and you are in the country of your enemies; then the land will rest and enjoy its Sabbaths.*

> *All the time that it lies desolate, the land will have the rest it did not have during the Sabbaths you lived in it.*
>
> (Leviticus 26:33–35 NIV)

In other words, Israel refused to keep the Sabbath of the land, so God said, "All right, I'll turn you out of the land, and the land will have nothing but Sabbaths all the time you are out of it, because you wouldn't observe the Sabbath when you were in it."

I've come to see that God deals with Christians in the same way. We're so busy and so active doing things for God that when God says, "Take time off, relax, rest, get alone, get away from everything because I have things I need to tell you," we are too busy to listen. I can think of men whom I could name – friends of mine – to whom God went on speaking and warning, but who would not listen. Finally, God said, "All right, you'll be in a hospital bed for twelve months. Then you'll have to rest!"

My personal conviction is that it's better to rest voluntarily than to be compelled to rest. i've made a personal decision to try to do that. I think there is a great deal of importance in taking time to relax, rest and wait upon God, and often to combine that rest with fasting. Then your spirit and your stomach rest. Your whole body gets a rest, as well as your whole personality.

Let me point out to you that God ordained a combination of fasting and resting for the Day of Atonement. Leviticus records God's ordinances for that day:

> *"This shall be a statute forever for you: In the seventh month, on the tenth day of the month, you shall afflict your souls, and do no work at all, whether a native of your own country or a stranger who dwells among you.*
>
> *For on that day the priest shall make atonement for you, to cleanse you, that you may be clean from all your sins before the Lord.*
>
> *It is a Sabbath of solemn rest for you, and you shall afflict your souls. It is a statute forever.*
>
> (Leviticus 16:29–31)

The priest had his part to do – he had to go into the Holy of Holies with the blood of the sacrifice and make propitiation for the sins of the people. However, the people had their part to do, and their part was twofold:

(1) to fast, and (2) to abstain from all work.

I feel the Lord is emphasizing that we unite these two things again. When we fast, if possible, we need to take time off from every other activity – not necessarily a whole day, but half a day – and set that time aside for God. Let our busy minds stop turning over for a little while. We're so busy, even when we pray, that we never give God a chance to tell us what to do. Praying is not just telling God, it's also listening to God. Sometimes it takes a good many hours to get into the position where we can hear Him. So I believe that rest should be linked with fasting.

Let me give you one other Scripture where fasting is united with taking a Sabbath. in the book of Joel, the people of God were faced with a tremendous crisis. They have no answer, so God told them His answer through the prophet Joel: "*Consecrate a fast, Call a sacred assembly; Gather the elders and all the inhabitants of the land into the house of the Lord your God, and cry out to the Lord.*" (Joel 1:14). A sacred assembly means a day when nobody does anything but seek God.

Years ago when we were in Jerusalem, during times of upheaval in the city, a curfew would be proclaimed, and the word they used at those times for curfew is the same word that is used in this passage for "a sacred assembly." A curfew is a time when no one is allowed out. Everybody has to stay at home. in other words, there is a voluntary restraint on all activities.

God tells us to sanctify a fast, proclaim a sacred assembly, stop our own activities, and set aside time for Him. in Joel 2:15–16 God said, "Blow the trumpet in Zion, Consecrate a fast, Call a sacred assembly; Gather the people, Sanctify the congregation, Assemble the elders, Gather the children," everyone was to stop all their own activities and take time to seek God.

11

How Should I Break a Fast?

One final concern as we close this study is with breaking a fast. This is a very important aspect of fasting. You may lose a lot of the benefits that are due you from fasting if you break your fast unwisely.

Some of us don't realize that the word "breakfast," which we still use in the English language, means the meal that breaks a fast. However, some people eat so much so late at night that they never have a fast to break. After fasting, always begin with a light meal, even if you have fasted only a short period of time. Don't begin with anything cooked or greasy or fat or heavy. Preferably begin with a raw salad or fruit. My experience has been that if you begin with a salad – especially lettuce or raw greens – it does a tremendous purging job on your whole body. it's like a brush, sweeping out your intestines. This has been my experience in breaking a fast this way.

The next thing to bear in mind is that the longer the fast, the more gradually you must break it. Somebody has said that you must take as long to break your fast as you spent fasting. I don't think that is completely accurate, but I have discovered when I fasted a long time (over three weeks) that my stomach was like a baby's. I had to be as careful about feeding myself after that fast as I would have been feeding a baby. it took me a week, at least, to get back to normal food.

This is where you are going to have to have real self-control. When you are in a fast, after about the first two or three days you don't feel hungry, but when you start to eat again, your hunger comes back. That is when you really must hold onto yourself. You may get mental pictures of all sorts of things you love eating, but you just can't give way because you can ruin many of the physical benefits of fasting by breaking your fast rapidly or unwisely.

One more point needs to be mentioned. As a result of fasting – even if it's only a couple of days – your stomach will have contracted. it is usually not wise to expand it again to the same extent. Most people in Western civilization have over-expanded stomachs. You will find that as you start eating after a fast, you will begin to feel full sooner than you would have before you fasted. Habit will make you go on eating the rest of the meal, but wisdom says, "Why not stop there? You've had enough."

Thus, fasting is a way also to change our eating habits, which many of us need to do. However, if you are planning to slim down or reduce, fasting alone will not do that normally. You will get a few pounds off, but you'll put them on just as quickly unless you combine it with a changed program of eating.

12

In Summary

In this study, we have covered many of the practical aspects of fasting. Briefly, in review, we defined fasting as abstaining from food for spiritual purposes. We saw that fasting is the revealed will of God and that He has promised to reward those who diligently seek Him through the scriptural way of fasting.

We also discovered several scriptural objects for fasting:

- To humble ourselves
- To come closer to God
- To help us understand God's Word
- To find God's will and to receive direction in our lives

- To seek healing or deliverance from evil spirits
- To seek God's intervention in some particular crisis or some problem which cannot be handled by ordinary means
- To intercede and pray on behalf of others

We also pointed out that our motive for fasting is much more important than the length of time we spend fasting. For those who have not fasted before, it is wise to begin with a shorter time and build up to longer periods of fasting.

During our periods of fasting, we need to take extra time for Bible study and prayer, guard against spiritual attack, and avoid religious ostentation. Because of the way we live today, we also pointed out that most people may experience some physical reactions during the early stages of a fast. Such reactions are usually a sign that our blood is doing a badly needed clean-up job on various parts of our body.

We also showed the parallel between fasting and the Sabbath, encouraging the combination of rest and relaxation with fasting and waiting upon God.

Finally, we covered how to break a fast so as to get the maximum physical benefits from it.

Fasting is both our duty and our privilege as Christians. Let us heed God's call to pray and fast, individually and corporately, trusting Him that He will fulfill His promise to reward those who diligently seek Him.

Part 2

Date: ________________

Today, I'm praying and fasting for:

____

____

____

____

____

____

Date: ________________

How my prayer has been answered:

____

____

____

____

____

____

For whatever is born of God overcomes the world, and this is the victory that has overcome the world – our faith.

(1 John 5:4)

Date: ________________

Today, I'm praying and fasting for:

____

____

____

____

____

____

Date: ________________

How my prayer has been answered:

____

____

____

____

____

____

The people who really rule the world are those who know how to pray.

Derek Prince

Date: ____________________

Today, I'm praying and fasting for:

____

____

____

____

____

____

Date: ____________________

How my prayer has been answered:

____

____

____

____

____

____

Blessed be God, who has not turned away my prayer, nor His mercy from me.

Psalm 66:20

Date: ________________

Today, I'm praying and fasting for:

____

____

____

____

____

____

Date: ________________

How my prayer has been answered:

____

____

____

____

____

____

Fasting deals with the two great barriers to the Holy Spirit that are erected by man's carnal nature. These are the stubborn self-will of the soul and the insistent self-gratifying appetites of the body.

Derek Prince

Date: ________________

Today, I'm praying and fasting for:

____

____

____

____

____

____

Date: ________________

How my prayer has been answered:

____

____

____

____

____

____

Submit yourselves, then, to God. Resist the devil, and he will flee from you.

James 4:7

Date: ____________________

Today, I'm praying and fasting for:

____

____

____

____

____

____

Date: ____________________

How my prayer has been answered:

____

____

____

____

____

____

Carnal weapons are of no use whatever for spiritual warfare. You cannot blast demons and rebellious angels out of the way with a tank.

Derek Prince

Date: ________________

Today, I'm praying and fasting for:

____

____

____

____

____

____

Date: ________________

How my prayer has been answered:

____

____

____

____

____

____

Thanks be to God! He gives us the victory through our Lord Jesus Christ.

1 Corinthians 15:57

Date: ____________________

Today, I'm praying and fasting for:

____

____

____

____

____

____

Date: ____________________

How my prayer has been answered:

____

____

____

____

____

____

We need to understand God doesn't just tolerate us, his favour is upon us. He is passionately committed to us. We never have any reason to doubt our access to Him.

Derek Prince

Date: ________________

Today, I'm praying and fasting for:

____

____

____

____

____

____

Date: ________________

How my prayer has been answered:

____

____

____

____

____

____

I believe that God exists and that He rewards me when I earnestly seek Him.

Hebrews 11:6

Date: ________________

Today, I'm praying and fasting for:

____

____

____

____

____

____

Date: ________________

How my prayer has been answered:

____

____

____

____

____

____

It is God's will for me to fast, and God will bless me when I do fast in accordance with His will.

Derek Prince

Date: ________________

Today, I'm praying and fasting for:

____

____

____

____

____

____

Date: ________________

How my prayer has been answered:

____

____

____

____

____

____

I sought the Lord, and he answered me; he delivered me from all my fears. Those who look to him are radiant; their faces are never covered with shame.

Psalm 34:4–5

Date: ________________

Today, I'm praying and fasting for:

____

____

____

____

____

____

Date: ________________

How my prayer has been answered:

____

____

____

____

____

____

I believe that God will reward me in fasting if I seek Him with right motives, biblically and with a humble heart.

Date: ________________

Today, I'm praying and fasting for:

____

____

____

____

____

____

Date: ________________

How my prayer has been answered:

____

____

____

____

____

____

God has chosen to dwell in the physical bodies of those who believe in Him. Thus, my body has a very important function as a residence of the Holy Spirit.

Date: ____________________

Today, I'm praying and fasting for:

____

____

____

____

____

____

Date: ____________________

How my prayer has been answered:

____

____

____

____

____

____

Blessed is the one who trusts in the Lord, whose confidence is in him.

Jeremiah 17:7

Date: ________________

Today, I'm praying and fasting for:

____

____

____

____

____

____

Date: ________________

How my prayer has been answered:

____

____

____

____

____

____

Therefore the Lord longs to be gracious to you, and therefore He waits on high to have compassion on you. For the Lord is a God of justice; how blessed are all those who long for Him.

Isaiah 30:18

About the Author

Derek Prince (1915–2003) was born in India of British parents. Educated as a scholar of Greek and Latin at Eton College and Cambridge University, England, he held a Fellowship in Ancient and Modern Philosophy at King's College. He also studied several modern languages, including Hebrew and Aramaic, at Cambridge University and the Hebrew University in Jerusalem.

While serving with the British army in World War II, he began to study the Bible and experienced a life-changing encounter with Jesus Christ. Out of this encounter he formed two conclusions: first, that Jesus Christ is alive; second, that the Bible is a true, relevant, up-to-date book. These conclusions altered the whole course of his life, which he then devoted to studying and teaching the Bible.

Derek's main gift of explaining the Bible and its teaching in a clear and simple way has helped build a foundation of faith in millions of lives. His non-denominational, non-sectarian approach has made his teaching equally relevant and helpful to people from all racial and religious backgrounds.

He is the author of over 50 books, 600 audio and 100 video teachings, many of which have been translated and published in more than 100 languages. His daily radio broadcast is translated into Arabic, Chinese (Amoy, Cantonese, Mandarin, Shanghainese, Swatow), Croatian, German, Malagasy, Mongolian, Russian, Samoan, Spanish and Tongan. The radio program continues to touch lives around the world.

Derek Prince Ministries persists in reaching out to believers in over 140 countries with Derek's teachings, fulfilling the mandate to keep on "until Jesus returns." This is effected through the outreaches of more than 45 Derek Prince offices around the world, including primary work in Australia, Canada, China, France, Germany, the Netherlands, New Zealand, Norway, Russia, SouthAfrica, Switzerland, the United Kingdom and the United States. For current information about these and other worldwide locations, visit www.derekprince.com.

ALSO RECOMMENDED FOR YOU

SHAPING HISTORY THROUGH PRAYER AND FASTING

Christians have altered the course of history and governments by emphasizing biblical methods of prayer and fasting.

Best-selling author and Bible teacher Derek Prince recounts from personal experience how history was shaped through prayer during the Second World War in North Africa, the birth of the State of Israel, the end of the Stalin era, and the independence of Kenya, East Africa.

Learn how you can implement change – in your family, church, locale, country, and the world.

Paperback and ebook
978-1-782633-10-5
£ 7.99

www.dpmuk.org/shop

ALSO RECOMMENDED FOR YOU

SPIRITUAL WARFARE FOR THE END TIMES

As the time approaches for Jesus' return, the spiritual battle between good and evil is heating up. The enemy is on the move.

Yet God is on the move, too, in powerful ways – and you can join Him in His work.

With piercing insight and practical application, Derek Prince will help you understand not only the intensified warfare environment in which we live, but also how you can help unleash God's goodness in the world.

Paperback and ebook
978-1-78263-470-6
£ 8.99

www.dpmuk.org/shop

ALSO RECOMMENDED FOR YOU

YOU SHALL RECEIVE POWER

The baptism in the Holy Spirit is a topic of constant interest, debate and even controversy among Christians around the world. Derek Prince thoroughly examines what the Word of God teaches on the subject and explains both the nature and the purpose of the baptism in the Holy Spirit.

In the second part of the book Prince focuses on the Holy Spirit's role as a Guide and learns you how to be led by the Spirit, how to live in God's grace, how to cooperate with the Holy Spirit's working in our life and how to hear God's voice.

Paperback and ebook
978-1-78263-442-3
£ 6.99

www.dpmuk.org/shop

MORE BEST-SELLERS BY DEREK PRINCE

Blessing Or Curse: You Can Choose

Called To Conquer

Destiny Of Israel And The Church, The

Foundational Truths For Christian Living

God's Remedy For Rejection

Life-Changing Spiritual Power

Marriage Covenant

Prayers & Proclamations

Prophetic Guide To The End Times

Rediscovering God's Church

Secrets Of A Prayer Warrior

They Shall Expel Demons

Who Is The Holy Spirit?

Derek Prince Ministries Offices Worldwide

DPM – Asia/Pacific
38 Hawdon Street
Sydenham
Christchurch 8023
New Zealand
T: + 64 3 366 4443
E: admin@dpm.co.nz
W: www.dpm.co.nz and www.derekprince.in

DPM – Australia
15 Park Road
Seven Hills
New South Wales 2147
Australia
T: +61 2 9838 7778
E: enquiries@au.derekprince.com
W: www.derekprince.com.au

DPM – Canada

P.O. Box 8354 Halifax
Nova Scotia B3K 5M1
Canada
T: + 1 902 443 9577
E: enquiries.dpm@eastlink.ca
W: www.derekprince.org

DPM – France

B.P. 31, Route d'Oupia
34210 Olonzac
France
T: + 33 468 913872
E: info@derekprince.fr
W: www.derekprince.fr

DPM – Germany

Söldenhofstr. 10
83308 Trostberg
Germany
T: + 49 8621 64146
E: ibl@ibl-dpm.net
W: www.ibl-dpm.net

DPM – Netherlands
Nijverheidsweg 12
7005 BJ Doetinchem
Netherlands
T: +31 251–255044
E: info@derekprince.nl
W: www.derekprince.nl

DPM – Norway
P.O. Box 129
Lodderfjord
N-5881 Bergen
Norway
T: +47 928 39855
E: sverre@derekprince.no
W: www.derekprince.no

Derek Prince Publications Pte. Ltd.
P.O. Box 2046
Robinson Road Post Office
Singapore 904046
T: + 65 6392 1812
E: dpmchina@singnet.com.sg
W: www.dpmchina.org (English)
www.ygmweb.org (Chinese)

DPM – South Africa
P.O. Box 33367
Glenstantia
0010 Pretoria
South Africa
T: +27 12 348 9537
E: enquiries@derekprince.co.za
W: www.derekprince.co.za

DPM – Switzerland
Alpenblick 8
CH-8934 Knonau
Switzerland
T: + 41 44 768 25 06
E: dpm-ch@ibl-dpm.net
W: www.ibl-dpm.net

DPM – UK
PO Box 393
Hitchin SG5 9EU
United Kingdom
T: + 44 1462 492100
E: enquiries@dpmuk.org
W: www.dpmuk.org

DPM – USA

P.O. Box 19501
Charlotte NC 28219
USA
T: + 1 704 357 3556
E: ContactUs@derekprince.org
W: www.derekprince.org

Lightning Source UK Ltd.
Milton Keynes UK
UKHW050613071219
354840UK00030B/824/P

9 781782 635635